IMAGES
of America

KNOTT'S BERRY FARM
THE EARLY YEARS

WALTER AND CORDELIA KNOTT, 1955. Walter Knott's grandparents had come to California from Texas via the covered wagon, so it is apropos that Knott and his wife, Cordelia, took time to pose in the covered wagon inside the Pitchur Gallery. (Orange County Archives.)

ON THE COVER: CALICO SQUARE, 1965. On a typical day at Knott's Berry Farm in 1965, train engineers inspect the No. 40 steam engine in Calico Square before its next departure. Meanwhile, children enjoy the Burro Rides, as visitors take a journey through the deep caverns of the Calico Mine Ride. (Author's collection.)

IMAGES
of America

KNOTT'S BERRY FARM
THE EARLY YEARS

Jay Jennings

ARCADIA
PUBLISHING

Published by Arcadia Publishing
Charleston, South Carolina

Printed in the United States of America

Library of Congress Control Number: 2009920011

For all general information contact Arcadia Publishing at:
Telephone 843-853-2070
Fax 843-853-0044
E-mail sales@arcadiapublishing.com
For customer service and orders:
Toll-Free 1-888-313-2665

Visit us on the Internet at www.arcadiapublishing.com

This book is dedicated, first and foremost, to Walter and Cordelia Knott, and the entire Knott family. It is also dedicated to the love of my life, Maria, and to my parents, Lou and Gloria, for all their love and support.

CONTENTS

ACKNOWLEDGMENTS

The early history of Knott's Berry Farm is an important chapter in the history of Southern California amusement parks. Having grown up in the 1970s, a good chunk of my childhood was spent at Knott's, walking up and down Ghost Town, talking to the street performers, and eating countless meals at the Chicken Dinner Restaurant.

Besides my interest in filmmaking, I have spent over 25 years researching the people and attractions associated with Knott's Berry Farm, including the Knott family themselves and their sheer will and determination to make everything they attempted in life a success.

During my years of research, I have accumulated a large collection of vintage Knott's Berry Farm memorabilia and photographs, which in itself has assisted in me in learning more about the farm and its Old West roots.

Over the years, I have become friends with many Knott family members and old-time Knott's Berry Farm employees, spending countless hours transcribing their memories and input on how the farm operated and what went on there.

I feel fortunate to be working with Arcadia Publishing, especially Debbie Seracini, in putting together this book of rare images that help tell the story of Knott's Berry Farm in the hopes of preserving its history for many generations to come.

I would like to thank the following people who helped make this book possible: Steve Knott, Marion Knott, Don Oliphant, Dean Davisson, Dave Bourne, Anita Calderonello, Richard Harris, and Chris Jepsen.

Unless otherwise credited, all photographs are from the author's personal collection; courtesy lines for the Orange County Archives are denoted as OCA.

FOREWORD

As a young child, I always loved Knott's Berry Farm. One of the reasons was the excitement of the Old West and all of the cowboys and Indians of the 1800s. I started working at Knott's opening and closing the doors at the Chapel by the Lake and was paid 10¢ an hour. I knew I could do that job—I was 10 years old. I moved on to clerk in our General Store, where we sold hams, block cheese, and penny candy. I became a sweeper at the age of 16 and was now a real employee with an identification card, and I paid taxes.

About this same time, during the summer before the sun came up, I would pick up live chickens from chicken farms for processing so that the Chicken Dinner Restaurant would have the freshest chickens possible for our guests. Later I was assigned to the preserving department and made jam and preserves. Then I went to the grounds crew and took care of the lawns, lakes, and trees, and even cleaned Beach Boulevard of all the trash from some of our guests from Orangethorpe Avenue to Lincoln Avenue.

My next job was a parking attendant, then clerk in the Berry Market, where I also sold jam and took fried chicken orders to go. All of these jobs that I worked were on the weekends, except when school was out in the summer, and then it was full time. I went to Arizona State University but returned each summer, working in the Steak House as a host and food quality coordinator.

The U.S. Army called, so I requested for draft, but instead of going to Germany, the army sent me to New Jersey, where I became a military policeman. When I got out of the army, I went to the Orange County Sheriff's Academy for additional police training and then attended Cal State Long Beach for certification as a polygraph examiner.

I moved into my new job at Knott's as a security officer. In a few years, I began running that department, and no, my last name did not hurt me in my promotion. Next I was a general partner, and I took control of many departments. Security, parking control, janitorial services, first aid, safety, concessions, the admission department, and more. It was great fun to work with my family, grandparents, parents, aunts, uncles, my brother, and cousins. I was chairman of the board off and on in my career. We rotated that position with family members of my generation.

I enjoyed every day at Knott's, and I do not remember one day that I did not want to go to work. There were so many good employees, and they were all good friends. To this day, I am still close to many former employees. I have had a great life at Knott's Berry Farm and am so proud to have been a part of it and to have the last name of Knott.

—Steve Knott
Grandson of Walter Knott

WALTER KNOTT, 1960. Walter Knott was the founder of Knott's Berry Farm.

INTRODUCTION

Knott's Berry Farm is one of the most famous amusement parks in the world, with a storied history that goes as far back as 1889, the year its founder, Walter Knott, was born. This book, through the use of rare photographs, will focus on the farm's early years: its development, attractions, street performers, restaurants, shops, employees, and of course, the Knott family.

First, here is some background information to help fully understand the significance of Knott's Berry Farm and its many historic moments and changes throughout the years.

In 1923, Walter Knott, a simple farmer, and his wife, Cordelia, started selling their berries from a roadside berry stand to passing cars on Highway 39 in Buena Park, California. They opened a small tearoom and berry market where they sold jams, jellies, juices, and pies in 1928, christening the area Knott's Berry Place. A few years later, in 1932, Knott developed a new berry, a cross between a red raspberry, blackberry, and loganberry. He named it the boysenberry in honor of its original cultivator, Rudolph Boysen. In 1934, Walter Knott's first successful crop of boysenberries were harvested and sold at the farm in jams, jellies, punch, and pies, all of which became the Knott family trademark.

In that same year, Cordelia Knott, trying to make ends meet during the Great Depression, served her first eight chicken dinners on her wedding china for 65¢. They proved to be so popular that Walter Knott decided to expand their tearoom and build the Chicken Dinner Restaurant, complete with separate kitchen, dining rooms, and parking lot. The restaurant opened in 1938, and word spread fast about Cordelia's delicious food, resulting in very long lines.

In 1940, a notable event occurred. In an attempt to entertain the thousands of restaurant customers lining up each day, Walter Knott hit upon the idea of building a real-life ghost town. In the next couple years, he relocated the Gold Trails Hotel (built in 1868) to Knott's Berry Place from Prescott, Arizona. In the hotel's lobby, he added the Covered Wagon Show. These new additions, along with a few early attractions such as Down by the Old Mill Stream and George Washington's Fireplace Replica, helped form the basis for his Knott's Ghost Town.

Throughout the late 1930s and early 1940s, Knott's Berry Place was a tightly run family business, with each of Walter Knott's children (Virginia, Russell, Marion, and Toni) taking on the responsibility of running different aspects of the farm: Russell Knott ran the Berry Market, Virginia Knott the Gift Shop, and Marion and Toni Knott the Dress and Sports Shop. Even their spouses were integrated into the family business. Toni's husband, Ken Oliphant, ran the jam and jelly department, whereas Virginia's husband, Ken Reafsnyder, ran the purchasing and publicity department. Marion's husband, Dwight "Andy" Anderson, was brought in to run the Steak House and the Ghost Town Grill.

Knott's Berry Place was officially renamed Knott's Berry Farm and Ghost Town in late 1947, and by the time the 1950s rolled around, the area was made up of dozens of entertaining attractions and shops, such as the Little Chapel by the Lake, the General Merchandise Store, the Post Office, the Blacksmith Shop, the Haunted Shack, the Calico Saloon, the Stagecoach Ride, the Wagon Camp, Panning for Gold, and Boot Hill Cemetery.

In 1951, Walter Knott bought America's last operating narrow-gauge railroad, the Denver and Rio Grande, and moved it in its entirety to Knott's Berry Farm.

During the 1940s and 1950s, a dubious cast of street performers roamed up and down Ghost Town, entertaining visitors and posing for pictures. Chief Red Feather, Dude Sands, Prospector Roy Bryant, Slim Vaughn, and Dad Lewis were among the most memorable. Not to be outdone, Handsome Brady and Whiskey Bill (two statues) sat on a bench outside the Gold Trails Hotel, attracting large crowds in their own right. The same can be said for the Calico Belle statues, Marilyn and Cecelia, who were located at the end of Ghost Town toward Calico Square. However, unlike their male counterparts, Marilyn and Cecelia were actual performers in the Calico Saloon. Another well-liked attraction was the amusing "Peek-Ins" (propped-up mannequins), which were on display inside old buildings all over Ghost Town. Among them were Wing Lee Laundry, One Eyed Ike in the Barber Shop, and Sad Eye Joe in jail.

It goes without saying that a talented crew of artists and designers working behind the scenes were chiefly responsible for bringing Ghost Town to life. Among them were Paul Swartz (art director), Paul von Klieben (designer), Claude Bell (sculptor), and Andy Anderson (wood carver), not to mention all the dedicated builders and engineers who worked alongside them.

In the years to come, more rides and attractions were added to Knott's Ghost Town (thanks to designer Bud Hurlbut), such as the Calico Mine Ride in 1960, which was designed to show visitors how gold was first mined. To honor our country's independence, Walter Knott built Independence Hall in 1966, complete with an exact replica of the cracked Liberty Bell. A few years later, the Calico Log Ride made its debut in 1969, and John Wayne attended the opening ceremonies. Later that year, Fiesta Village was added as a tribute to California's early Spanish heritage. After that, the short-lived Gypsy Camp was built in 1971, as was the 2,100-seat John Wayne Theatre, where California governor Ronald Reagan presided over the celebrity-filled opening gala. Over the years, the theater would attract top-named entertainers and singers, such as Duke Ellington, Tom Jones, Pat Boone, Debbie Reynolds, Lou Rawls, and Kenny Rogers. In 1975, the Roaring Twenties–themed area made its debut and introduced its first roller coaster, Corkscrew, as well as the more leisurely paced Knott's Bear-y Tales. For even more thrills, the Parachute Sky Jump and Sky Cabin, nearly 20 stories high, were later added in 1976.

There is no doubt that during these early years, the seeds of Knott's Berry Farm's legacy were deeply planted, thanks to a simple farmer with a fondness for the Old West and a vision to honor America's past.

One

THE EARLY YEARS OF WALTER KNOTT

ROSAMOND DOUGHERTY, 1860s. In 1849, Walter Knott's grandmother, Rosamond Dougherty, along with her husband, Charles, journeyed from Virginia to Texas. In 1868, after years of disillusionment, almost penniless, and caring for their young daughter, Virginia, they loaded their belongings and family into a covered wagon and began the trek west by wagon train, traveling to Southern California by way of the Colorado River and finally settling on a new farm near the foothills surrounding the cities of Azusa, Glendora, and Covina.

COVERED WAGON JOURNEY, 1868. The covered wagon journey that Walter Knott's grandparents took in 1868 (depicted in a sketch drawing by Paul von Klieben) would later have a huge impact on him, as would the stories his grandmother told him about his uncle John King, sheriff of San Bernardino County from 1879 to 1882 and one of the last, great frontier marshals who organized posses to take up the trail of criminals across the largest county in the United States.

ELGIN AND VIRGINIA KNOTT, 1887. In 1887, Elgin Knott, a minister from Tennessee, came to California, where he courted and married Virginia Dougherty. Because of his ailing health, his doctor advised him to stay in California, where he started a church near Newport Beach.

LITTLE WALTER KNOTT. On December 11, 1889, Elgin and Virginia Knott's first son, Walter Knott, was born in San Bernardino, California. In 1896, after an accidental fall from a train step that badly injured his lung, Elgin Knott died.

VIRGINIA KNOTT AND SONS, 1900. Times were hard for Virginia Knott and her two sons, Elgin Jr. and Walter. In 1899, she sold the 60 acres of land that her husband had left her and moved her family to Pomona, California. Around 1900, ten-year-old Walter Knott raised vegetables on vacant lots, selling the produce in the morning before school, and delivered newspapers in the evenings to help supplement the family income.

13

WALTER KNOTT GETS MARRIED, 1911. In 1910, Walter Knott took a job as a construction foreman. It paid well enough that he was able to build a house in Pomona, California (which still stands today at 1040 West Fourth Street). On June 3, 1911, Knott married his Pomona High School sweetheart, Cordelia Hornaday.

STARTING A FAMILY, 1914. In 1914, Walter Knott moved his wife and young daughter, Virginia, to a homestead near Newberry Springs, out on the Mojave Desert beyond Barstow. Unfortunately, farming proved almost impossible in the dry desert valley. While Cordelia Knott stayed behind in their little adobe home to look after Virginia, Walter Knott was forced to find other work. (OCA.)

THE KNOTT CHILDREN, 1922. By 1922, Walter and Cordelia Knott had three more children, totaling four altogether. From left to right are Elizabeth (Toni), Marion, Virginia, and Russell. A few years earlier, Walter Knott took a job at the famous old desert mining town of Calico in San Bernardino, where a group of promoters hoped to work through the old tailings and extract the remaining silver. (OCA.)

WALTER KNOTT MOVES TO SHANDON, 1920. In 1920, Walter Knott received 160 acres from the government to improve his homestead. Still wanting to be a farmer, Knott turned down a chance to return to his old contracting job in Pomona. Instead he went to work for one of his cousins and became a tenant farmer, growing crops to feed the ranch hands and living near the little town of Shandon in northern San Luis Obispo County. (OCA.)

YOUNG WALTER AND CORDELIA KNOTT, 1920s. After three years of hard work, the Knotts had $2,500 in the bank. With the Knott children getting older, Walter Knott started looking for a new opportunity near a bigger town with better schools. Cordelia Knott also supplemented the family income by making and selling homemade candy. (OCA.)

WALTER KNOTT JOINS JIM PRESTON IN BUENA PARK, 1920. In 1920, Walter Knott joined his cousin, Jim Preston, in a partnership that saw the two of them growing berries together at a place called Buena Park. The company of Preston and Knott leased 20 acres of land along Grand Avenue from William Coughran. It was a five-year deal with a possible two-year extension. The rent was $50 an acre. While Preston was the senior partner, it was clear that Knott (above) was the one on the ground, doing the work.

ROADSIDE BERRY STAND, 1923. In 1923, while looking for ways to bring in more money, Walter Knott decided to start selling the berries he had harvested directly to the public from a small roadside stand 22 miles south of Los Angeles on California State Highway 39, later Beach Boulevard. (Above, OCA.)

HARVESTING BERRIES, 1924. The advance blackberry was Preston and Knott's first big variety. It ripened by mid-April 1924, up to three weeks before most other varieties. By this time, they had 19 acres just in advance blackberries, along with 3 acres of red raspberries, 3 acres of strawberries, 3 acres of dewberries, 2 acres of loganberries, and 2 acres of Macatawa blackberries. (OCA.)

HARD WORK PAYS OFF, 1925. During the harvest season of 1925, the farm had as many as 50 pickers working at once, but none worked harder than Walter Knott (inside truck). (OCA.)

PICKING RHUBARB, 1927. By 1927, Preston and Knott (far left) were pushing the youngberry very hard, selling both fruit and rootstock throughout Southern California, Arizona, and New Mexico. Besides berries, they also added other crops, including asparagus and cherry rhubarb. (OCA.)

TYING UP BERRY VINES, 1927. Rhubarb was a good producer by 1927, sometimes yielding four crops a year, and it was also a good rotation crop for the berry vines that Walter Knott (far right) and his workers would tie up in the fields, even though they would tend to drop in production after a few years. (OCA.)

WALTER KNOTT: DETERMINED FARMER, 1927. The year 1927 marked the end of the lease in Buena Park, so Preston and Knott decided to end their partnership, but Walter Knott was determined to stay. Even though William Coughran had died two years before, Knott approached his son, Sam, with a proposition. He offered to buy 10 acres for $1,500 an acre, with plans to put up a pie-and-coffee room and berry market. The catch was that he could not pay any money down. (OCA.)

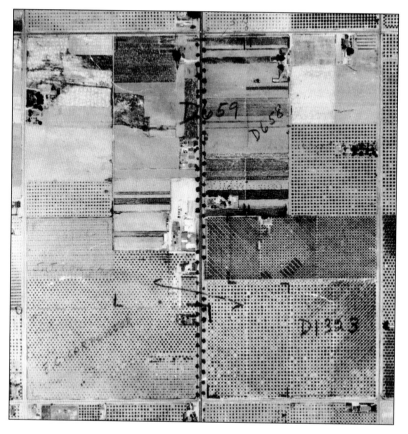

WALTER KNOTT'S NEW FARM, 1927. The interest on the land Walter Knott wanted to buy in 1927 was more than Preston and Knott had been paying in rent, but Knott was determined to have his own farm. This early aerial view depicts the land that would eventually become Knott's Berry Farm and Ghost Town. (OCA.)

Two

INTRODUCING KNOTT'S BERRY PLACE

KNOTT'S BERRY PLACE, 1928. In 1928, Walter Knott constructed a new building along Grand Avenue with a home for his family out back. The 80-foot stucco structure included a nursery on the south end, a berry market in the middle, and a tearoom with five tables on the north end with seating for 20. The Tea Room was where Cordelia sold sandwiches, fresh-baked rolls and jam, berry pie, and ice cream during the harvest season. The premises on which all of this stood were christened "Knott's Berry Place." (OCA.)

A Family Affair, 1928. All of the Knott children were expected to do their share of the work. The girls helped their mother in the Tea Room, while Russell Knott (left) worked for his father (right) in the berry business, both in the fields and in the Berry Market. In return, all of them were paid for their work, while Walter and Cordelia Knott only took cash when they needed it. (OCA.)

Selling Jams and Jellies, 1928. By 1928, the farm had more than 30 varieties of berries growing on 50 acres. Over the next two decades, the Berry Market sold canned berries in many forms, not to mention rhubarb, jams, jellies, and juices, which were put up in the farm's own preserving kitchen. The market also started selling fresh chicken, dried fruits, and a line of gift packs. (OCA.)

THE BERRY MARKET, 1930. All through the late 1920s and early 1930s, Walter Knott (at right, and below) was on the lookout for the next big berry. For years, he had been bringing in new varieties from all over the United States and some from foreign countries, and trying them out here, always with the hope of finding an outstanding new variety to sell to his customers at the Berry Market. (Both, OCA.)

RUDY BOYSEN, 1932. In 1932, George Darrow of the U.S. Department of Agriculture and Walter Knott went to see Rudolph Boysen, park superintendent in Anaheim, about his new berry, a cross between a blackberry, a loganberry, and a red raspberry. Boysen had planted them on his in-laws' ranch without any luck. He let Knott transplant a few scraggly plants to his farm, where they flourished. In 1933, Knott had his first crop of what he called the "boysenberry" in honor of its original cultivator, and it has been the Knott family trademark ever since.

WALTER AND RUSSELL KNOTT, 1934. With just 100 vines, Knott's Berry Place produced 2,200 baskets of boysenberries in 1934. The oversized berries, which Walter Knott and his son Russell sold in one-pound baskets, were returning more than $1,700 an acre.

THE FIRST CHICKEN DINNER, 1934. The Great Depression was dragging on, and money was still tight. To try to lure in more people, Cordelia Knott decided to expand her Tea Room menu by offering a home-cooked fried chicken dinner. So, in 1934, she served her first eight chicken dinners on her wedding china for 65¢ each, featuring a salad, vegetable, cherry rhubarb, and boysenberry pie for dessert. All the cooking was done in her home kitchen, and her chicken dinner was the only entrée on the menu. Later the Tea Room grew to seat 40 customers. (Both, OCA.)

BUILDING A RESTAURANT, 1937. In 1937, the Tea Room was expanded as Walter and Cordelia Knott oversaw the building of a genuine 225-seat Chicken Dinner Restaurant, complete with separate kitchen, dining rooms, and parking lot. Knott's daughter, Toni, hand-lettered and designed the first menus.

CHICKEN DINNER RESTAURANT, 1938. According to Walter Knott, when the Chicken Dinner Restaurant opened in 1938, he wrote a letter to all his customers and told them that now he had much more seating and a bigger kitchen, and that they would not have to wait in line anymore, but come the very first day, on the first weekend, they were all still waiting in line.

DINING ROOM, 1938. In 1938, during the Chicken Dinner Restaurant's first full year of operation, more than 265,000 chicken dinners were served in the dining rooms. The chickens were purchased from dozens of local ranchers and were raised to Cordelia Knott's exacting specifications. (OCA.)

CORDELIA'S KITCHEN, 1938. Cordelia Knott had 35 people working for her in the kitchen of the Chicken Dinner Restaurant in 1938, while her daughters managed a dining room staff of 55. Two more dining rooms were also added later that year. Now 400 diners could be seated at one time. (OCA.)

MAKING PIES, 1938. All the pies were made by hand in the Chicken Dinner Restaurant, with the gals in the kitchen pounding out the dough. They were sold only through the Knott's Bakery, Berry Market, and Farm Market. (OCA.)

LONG LINES, 1938. In 1938, as the crowds for the Chicken Dinner Restaurant grew and the lines lengthened (especially on Sundays and Mother's Day), Walter Knott began looking for ways to keep his guests occupied during the long wait. (OCA.)

ROCK GARDEN, 1938. Walter Knott and some of his workers started construction on the Rock Garden on the west side of the Chicken Dinner Restaurant in 1938. According to Knott, rock was the primary thing in the building of any rock garden, so he sent for 15 tons of volcanic specimens from Death Valley. (OCA.)

Down by the Old Mill Stream and George Washington's Fireplace, 1938. In 1938, Walter Knott built two early attractions near the Chicken Dinner Restaurant: a water wheel he called Down by the Old Mill Stream and a replica of George Washington's Mount Vernon fireplace, which the Knotts had admired while on vacation.

VIRGINIA'S GIFT SHOP, 1938. Walter Knott's oldest daughter, Virginia, started up a little gift shop in 1938 with just a few items on a card table at the north end of the Chicken Dinner Restaurant. Soon the gift shop became its own building, known as Virginia's Gift Shop, where one could find different kinds of trinkets and treasures, such as costume jewelry, ceramics, perfumes, American glass, German figurines, and original mementos from the Old West like powder horns, key chains, and coin purses. (Both, OCA.)

RESTAURANT EXPANSION, 1939. By 1939, the Chicken Dinner Restaurant expanded to 600 seats, including a new wing on the north side of the building to accommodate the large crowds. (Both, OCA.)

REGISTRATION ROOM, 1939. The Registration Room was built in 1939 as a place where diners could sign up for the Chicken Dinner Restaurant (and later for the Steak House and Ghost Town Grill) and be alerted via loudspeaker when their table was ready.

ACTIVE VOLCANO, 1939. The Active Volcano was built just outside the north end of the Chicken Dinner Restaurant in December 1939. According to Walter Knott, an unsightly standpipe stood 12 feet high, and there was no way to eliminate it. So he decided to make a 12-foot-tall volcano out of it, fully equipped with a boiler that rumbled, hissed, and spit steam at the push of a button, and put a desert cactus garden all around it. There was even a little red devil that turned the crank to make it go.

PLANTING TREES. The large eucalyptus trees around the farm were originally planted from gallon cans early in 1939. As the years went by, the two most often noticed examples of these trees were the one growing through the buggy on Main Street in front of the Post Office and the fine one growing on the dance floor at the Wagon Camp. Up until the 1960s, Walter Knott was still planting trees around the farm. (OCA.)

REDWOOD STUMP, 1939. Redwood Stump, a coast redwood tree that grew near Eureka, California, was moved to the farm, next to the Registration Room, in 1939. By counting the rings on this old stump, it has been revealed to be over 800 years old. A little sign in front pointed out the events that happened during the life of the tree. (OCA.)

OLD STAGECOACH, 1939. The Old Stagecoach came from Northern California and was placed next to the Active Volcano outside the Chicken Dinner Restaurant in 1939. This particular stagecoach was once robbed by Black Bart, the famous highwayman who robbed dozens of stages and always left little rhyming notes behind signed "Black Bart, the Po-8." (OCA.)

GHOST TOWN FIRE DEPARTMENT, 1939. In 1939, Knott's Berry Place experienced a couple of fires that could have been disastrous had they occurred near the dining rooms. Since there was no fire protection in the area, Clyde Finley (in the driver's seat), along with some other employees, formed the Ghost Town Fire Department. They became the first volunteer fire department in California under the Department of Forestry. (OCA.)

CORDELIA KNOTT, 1940. By 1940, the Chicken Dinner Restaurant was a huge success, serving as many as 4,000 dinners on Sunday evenings, and Cordelia Knott ran a tight kitchen, overseeing its entire operation up until the 1970s, even making and baking her own pies. (OCA.)

REALLY LONG LINES, 1940. Word of mouth spread fast about the Chicken Dinner Restaurant in 1940, so it was not unusual during those early years for customers to wait in long lines outside the restaurant, sometimes for three to four hours. (OCA.)

KEN OLIPHANT, 1942. In 1942, Ken Oliphant (far right) married Toni Knott. That same year, Oliphant had the idea to take Cordelia Knott's jam and jelly recipes right off the stove and make them into a larger batch to sell at the farm, so a tin building with pots and burners was built behind the Knott house, which was called Ken's Preserving Kitchen. Helping him in the kitchen were a loyal group of jam and jelly makers. (OCA.)

PRESERVING KITCHEN. As business grew, a full-scale Preserving Kitchen was built on the premises in 1966 and expanded into the parking lot area as the farm made and sold a line of jams, jellies, salad dressing, meat relish, and barbecue sauce. In the early 1960s, the Knott family got into grocery distribution, using food brokers to handle their delivery operation. (OCA.)

KEN REAFSNYDER, 1940S.
Ken Reafsnyder married
Virginia Knott in the early
1940s and ran the purchasing,
maintenance, and construction
departments during those
years. By 1951, he was the
farm's supervisor and operated
the Ghost Town Railroad.

GUY TESTER. Guy
Tester, who used
to babysit a young
Virginia Knott,
started working at
Knott's Berry Place
in 1946, becoming
Walter Knott's
right-hand man and
working there well
into the 1970s. He
was the director of
personnel, hiring
the employees and
creating most of the
street performers,
giving each one a
special niche. He
was also the editor
of the long-running
Knott's employee
newsletter, the
Knotty Post. (OCA.)

MARION AND TONI'S DRESS SHOP, 1946. Walter Knott's daughters, Marion and Toni, ran the Dress Shop (later Marion and Toni's Sport Shop), which was built in 1946 with logs and adobe bricks, and featured heavy eucalyptus beams. Originally, the shop sold custom-designed, tailored apparel and millinery, but the emphasis changed to sportswear, including a line of frocks, skirts, blouses, and casual wear, not to mention a variety of active sports togs, such as denims, pedal pushers, and jackets. (Right, OCA.)

GOLD TRAILS HOTEL, 1940. Walter Knott had always been fascinated with the pioneer days of the Old West. In 1940, Knott decided to build a two-story hotel on the corner of Market Street and Gold Mine Road called the Gold Trails Hotel (Old Trails Hotel), specifically to house a cyclorama, a three-dimensional curved painting with scenery and props built in front of it. The hotel was originally built in 1868 in a mining town near Prescott, Arizona; it was disassembled and rebuilt at Knott's Berry Place. It would be another two years before the hotel and cyclorama would be open to the public. (Both, OCA.)

Three

BUILDING A GHOST TOWN

WELCOME TO GHOST TOWN, 1940. In 1940, Walter Knott came up with a historic idea to build an entire Western ghost town at Knott's Berry Place to entertain the long lines of customers waiting to get into the Chicken Dinner Restaurant and at the same time pay homage to the pioneering spirit of his grandparents and his love of the Old West. So he began construction of the first street of Ghost Town Village, as it was originally known, wanting it to be both entertaining and educational. (OCA.)

PAUL SWARTZ AND GHOST TOWN CONSTRUCTION, 1940. As Walter Knott's concept for Ghost Town was coming together in 1940, a young artist named Paul Swartz arrived on the scene hoping to make a little money cutting silhouettes for the waiting crowds. He caught Knott's enthusiasm for Ghost Town and soon joined in on its design and construction, becoming its art director. (Both, OCA.)

WALTER KNOTT ON THE LOOKOUT, 1940. In 1940, every time he had the opportunity to get away for a couple of days, Walter Knott liked to visit the ghost towns and deserts of the west, seeking materials with which to reconstruct the ghost town at Knott's Berry Place. (OCA.)

GHOST TOWN RELICS, 1940. By securing a building here and part of another there, Walter Knott continually searched for authentic relics of the Gold Rush days, including furnishings to adorn the interiors of the old buildings in Ghost Town, as well as buying up old barns, buggies, wagons, tools, furniture, and anything else he could find to show life as it was lived in the early days. (OCA.)

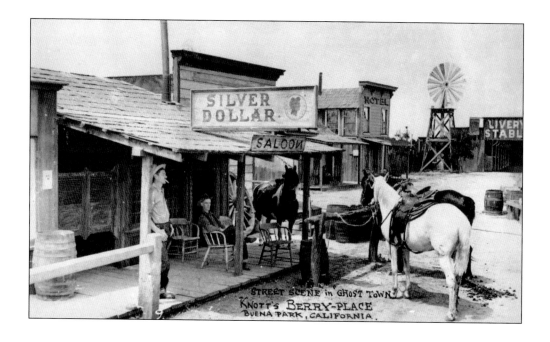

SILVER DOLLAR SALOON, 1940. The Silver Dollar Saloon was built in 1940 and was one of the first buildings in Ghost Town. Only soft drinks were served. Inside, visitors could read some of the humorous and ridiculous signs on the walls and look at a few objects reminiscent of an old-time saloon.

BLACKSMITH SHOP, 1940. Since blacksmith shops were important in every early pioneer town, one of the first shops put up in Ghost Town in 1940 was the Blacksmith Shop. It was not torn down and built up as many of the buildings were. It was simply moved to Knott's as is. When Walter Knott came to Buena Park in 1920 and started farming, this old blacksmith shop was standing on a farm not more than a mile from Ghost Town. Knott remembered the old shop and arranged to move it intact. Antique hinges, lamps, and other items were made in this shop. The farm's smithy (blacksmith) would be responsible for shoeing the Stage Coach horses that would later circle Ghost Town every day. (Below, OCA.)

GHOST TOWN JAIL AND ANDY ANDERSON, 1940. The Ghost Town Jail was built in 1940 and was copied after an old jail in an Arizona ghost town. Inside, Sad Eye Joe (right), a horse thief, sat in jail all by his lonesome, speaking to visitors and calling them by name when they walked by. Sad Eye Joe was one of many "peek-ins" (hand-carved wooden figures posing in various scenes) that woodcarver H. S. "Andy" Anderson (left) carved and built. Anderson had a studio in Santa Fe, New Mexico, where he also lived. (OCA.)

GOLDIE'S PLACE, 1940. Goldie's Place (or Goldie's Joint) was built in 1940 in front of the Ghost Town Jail. It was copied after an old building that Walter Knott had seen in Bodie, California, only days before so much of that town burned down. A woman's leg wearing a garter belt can be seen sticking out of Goldie's upper window. (OCA.)

SHERIFF'S OFFICE, 1940. The Sheriff's Office was built in 1940, right next door to Goldie's Place and the Ghost Town Jail. Inside the office were four hand-carved wooden figures (carved by Andy Anderson) gathered around a poker table. From left to right are Pat O'Leary, the Shady Gambler, the Sheriff, and Injun Joe.

WING LEE LAUNDRY, 1940. Wing Lee Laundry was built in 1940. In the early days of California mining, the Chinese settled in many California towns, running restaurants, laundries, and vegetable gardens. When Walter Knott was a boy, in every Western town, there were rows of Chinese shacks much like the one in Ghost Town. Inside, visitors could watch Hop Wing Lee (carved by Andy Anderson) wash clothes and sing songs.

ASSAY OFFICE, 1940. The Assay Office was built in 1940. As history goes, an assay office was an important and necessary part of every early-day mining camp. Here the ore was sampled and assayed, and fortunes were made or lost on the results of these assays. The assayer determined the amount of gold in a single ounce of the sample that was brought to him. Andy Anderson carved the assayer inside the office, sampling ore.

DEADWOOD DICK'S GRAVE, 1940s. Right in front of the Assay Office lies Deadwood Dick's Grave. Dick was an outlaw who thought he could outsmart the Sheriff, but instead, the Sheriff buried him.

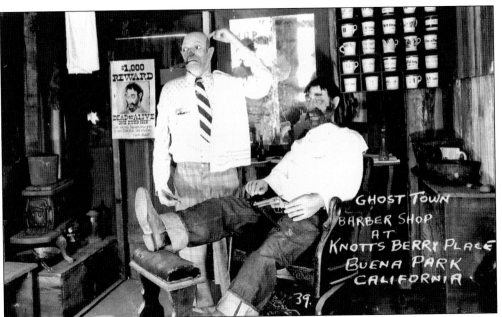

BARBER SHOP, 1940. The Barber Shop was built in 1940. Sam the Barber and One Eyed Ike were carved by Andy Anderson. There was a pained look on the barber's face, as it had just dawned on him that the rough customer in the chair with the gun on his lap was the same bandit described in the poster on the wall.

KNOTT'S LAKE, 1940. Knott's Lake (the Island) was made near the Berry Fields in 1940 after Walter Knott bought the land, which was once an alkali bed on a dairy farm that had been used for many years as a community dump. Knott got a big bulldozer, dug an immense hole in the center of the land, pushed all the trash over into the hole, and covered it up, thus making the Island. Then the rest of the alkali ground was made into the lake. (OCA.)

OLD WINDMILL AND LIVERY STABLE, 1940. The Old Windmill was brought to Ghost Town in 1940 and put up at the end of Main Street, which Walter Knott thought at the time was as far as Ghost Town was going. It was originally brought to Riverside from England by an English syndicate that laid out and subdivided Riverside in the 1860s. Next to the Old Windmill was the Livery Stable, which housed a unique collection of antique wagons, buggies, and carts. (Below, OCA.)

PITCHUR GALLERY, 1940. The Pitchur Gallery, built in 1940, was where hilarious pictures in the Old West motif were made of visitors in different poses, such as riding in a covered wagon, getting married, riding a bucking bronco, lifting weights, dancing with a sweetheart, and posing with Sad Eye Joe in jail. In addition, cameras could be bought or rented there, and film was sold and developed.

GUS THORNROSE, 1940. The Pitchur Gallery was a concession operated by Gus Thornrose and Paul Swartz, with Walter Knott only taking a small percentage. Thornrose was Knott's official photographer, even taking photographs of Ghost Town as it was being constructed. Later, in 1944, Clyde Finley helped run the Pitchur Gallery (which he ran until 1971). (OCA.)

GHOST TOWN NEWS AND PRINT SHOP, 1941. The Ghost Town News and Print Shop was built in 1941, when Knott's Berry Place began editing its own newspaper, the *Ghost Town News*, using an old Washington handpress like the one Benjamin Franklin used more than 150 years before. Walter Knott (below) would stop by on his horse quite often to give his input on what stories should be written. The shop would put visitors' names on old "Wanted" posters so they could show their friends—a real neat novelty at the time. (Above, OCA.)

LITTLE CHAPEL BY THE LAKE, 1941. The Little Chapel by the Lake was built in 1941 to house one of Paul von Klieben's most extraordinary paintings: a fluorescent portrait of Jesus Christ called *The Transfiguration*. Upon entering the chapel, visitors took a seat and heard a description of what Christ may have looked like. As the narration progressed, the altar doors containing the painting were fully opened, and with the black light shining upon the painting, it appeared that Christ's eyes were opening!

Betsy the Old Borax Engine, 1941. Betsy the Old Borax Engine was brought to Ghost Town in 1941 from Trona, California, where Walter Knott found it sitting on a little piece of track in the desert. This old wood-burning train engine was a favorite attraction among visitors, as it sat on Main Street, just past the Blacksmith Shop. (Above, OCA.)

COVERED WAGON SHOW, 1942. The Covered Wagon Show, featuring a large cyclorama painting commemorating Walter Knott's grandparents coming west from Texas in a covered wagon, opened inside the lobby of the Gold Trails Hotel in February 1942. The painting was started by artist Fritz Seelig and completed by renowned European designer Paul von Klieben. After visitors signed the guest book, they entered the main room and sat on benches to view the grandiose painting as the prerecorded narration began, recounting the hardships of Rosamond Dougherty's journey west. (Above, OCA.)

POST OFFICE, 1942. The Post Office was built in 1942 and for 10 years was just a dummy post office for looks. In 1952, it became a real post office with a postmaster, doing more than $30,000 a year in business for Uncle Sam. In June 1963, it closed as an official post office and became a "peek-in" with a postmaster inside carved by Andy Anderson.

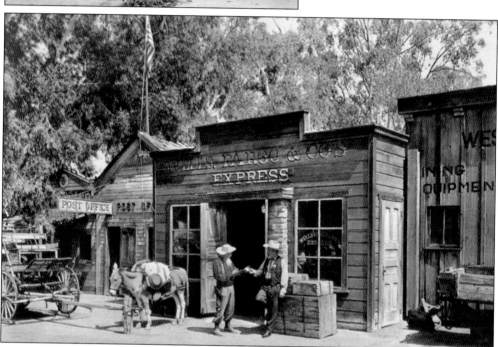

WELLS FARGO EXPRESS OFFICE, 1942. The Wells Fargo Express Office was built in 1942 right next to the Post Office. Wells Fargo was a business in California that dated back to the early days of the Gold Rush. These two buildings were typical of many post offices and express offices in old mining towns.

GENERAL MERCHANDISE STORE, 1944. The General Merchandise Store was first constructed in 1944. When the building was finished, it was not a replica of any specific building but was typical of the architecture of the Gold Rush days. The first merchandise obtained for stocking the store came from an old general store in Santa Barbara, California where old shoes, clothing, and nails were bought. (Above, OCA.)

GENERAL MERCHANDISE STORE INTERIOR, 1940S. Walter Knott bought even more fixtures from an old Santa Barbara store when the owner passed away and then used the remaining merchandise for his own General Merchandise Store. Later Knott bought out another old store in Maryland that had even older and more curious merchandise to add to his general store, including a potbellied stove.

PROSPECTOR'S ARASTRA, 1944. The Prospector's Arastra, a primitive gold mining mill turned by a burro to break up rock to recover the gold, was hauled to Ghost Town in 1944 from outside an abandoned mine between Baker and Death Valley. An old miner known only as Desert Jim used it for many years before his death.

BOTTLE HOUSE AND MUSIC HALL, 1945. The Bottle House was built in 1944. As in several of the early-day mining camps, it was made from more than 3,000 empty wine and whiskey bottles. The Music Hall was designed by Paul von Klieben in 1945 and was connected to the Bottle House. It was built to house the Knott family's collection of rare music boxes and mechanical music players. Charles Nahl's 1870 painting *Night Watch* was hung at the north end of the hall.

OLD LOGGING WHEELS, 1945. The Old Logging Wheels were first displayed next to the Music Hall in 1945. They were typical of those used in many logging camps before donkey engines made them obsolete. Anywhere from six to eight oxen were used to haul them.

PAUL VON KLIEBEN AND GHOST TOWN, 1940s. Paul von Klieben was responsible for a good portion of Ghost Town's artwork and design, taking tremendous pains in developing its details. Visitors could stroll through his Adobe Studio and watch him work. Walter Knott always praised him, attributing much of Ghost Town's success to von Klieben, who replaced Paul Swartz as art director. (Both, OCA.)

ART GLOW STUDIO, 1940s. The Art Glow Studio opened near Knott's Lake in the mid-1940s. In this unique shop, visitors walked through a veritable garden of flowers, birds, and other unique objects that, when the lights were turned out, reflected all the colors of the rainbow with translucent light. Inside, custom ceramics were handmade. The studio was operated by Lou Morris. (OCA.)

WOODCRAFT SHOP, 1940s. The Woodcraft Shop opened in the mid-1940s on Grand Avenue. Fine woods from the United States, Switzerland, Italy, and the South Seas were represented in the form of carvings, figurines, and decorative pieces for the home. Many carvings were done right there in the shop, which was operated by Ed Logan and Bill Yeaman. (OCA.)

DAD LEWIS, 1940s. Dad Lewis (Sheriff Lewis) joined Ghost Town in the mid-1940s and became one of its most memorable characters. Lewis was an established old vaudevillian, with a big old trunk of original costumes. He hung out all over Ghost Town and later in the Calico Saloon. He was known for wearing wooden-shoe clog boots with leather tops and dancing a soft-shoe jig in the middle of Main Street for large crowds of bystanders.

DUDE SANDS, 1940s. Dude Sands joined Ghost Town as a street performer in the mid-1940s and was a mainstay there until 1959. He was from Montana and spent most of his earlier life working with cattle. Sands worked all over Main Street and spent some time in the Print Shop. For a time he was also sheriff of Ghost Town. In 1956, a monument in Sands's likeness was built at the north entrance.

SLIM VAUGHN, 1940s. Slim Vaughn (left) worked in Ghost Town throughout the 1940s and 1950s, and was known as "the Village Romeo." He was a landscaper by trade who lived in Tujunga, California. He was a popular street performer who would pose for pictures and act out small skits, including being hung from a tree! He also participated in various Old West and forty-niner events throughout the Southland. (OCA.)

ED STROUS, 1940s. Many old prospectors worked the streets of Ghost Town during the 1940s and 1950s. One such old-timer was Ed Strous, who walked up and down Main Street with his mule and hung out at the Prospector's Arastra. (OCA.)

GUS BOYDSTON, 1940s. Gus Boydston was an old prospector who walked all over Ghost Town with his many mules during the 1940s and 1950s. Visitors could see him on Main Street and at the Prospector's Arastra.

DWIGHT "ANDY" ANDERSON, 1945. In 1945, Dwight "Andy" Anderson married Marion Knott, and a year later, Walter Knott asked him to run two new eateries, the Buffalo Steak House and the Ghost Town Grill. Later he would also develop two other eateries, Suter's Grub Steak and the Burger Wagon. (OCA.)

Glass Blower's Shop, 1946. The Glass Blower's Shop opened in 1946 and featured numerous items in spun or blown glass, with figurines, animals, and flowers in unusual designs and sparkling colors. The shop was operated by Harold Hacker. (OCA.)

Red's Leather Works, 1946. Red's Leather Works opened in 1946. Red Walker, who operated the shop, carried a fine stock of leather, suede, and hide items, and if visitors could not find what they wanted, he would make it for them. Western gear, shoes and various types of Native American footwear, tooled bags, belts, and billfolds were found there as well. The shop moved to Grand Avenue in 1953. (OCA.)

BUFFALO STEAK HOUSE, 1946. The Buffalo Steak House opened in 1946 under the watchful eye of Dwight "Andy" Anderson. The restaurant featured rustic furnishings, colorful Native American handicrafts, and a Western atmosphere with portraits of native chiefs on the walls, all designed and painted by Paul von Klieben. By June 1952, the steak house added the Garden Room, with an indoor garden and waterfall, followed by the Family Room, which contained a humorous mural depicting an American family at dinner. (Both, OCA.)

GHOST TOWN GRILL, 1946. The Ghost Town Grill opened in 1946. The grill's front counter was decorated like a covered wagon with a long mural of covered wagons adorning the walls. Patrons could also dine in an indoor patio with wooden tables and chairs where an old oxcart added to the Old West atmosphere. The manager of the grill was Ray Nelson. Ray's mother, Marie, was Walter Knott's longtime secretary. Red Walker's father, "Daddy" Mapes Walker, was the head chef. The grill was supervised by Dwight "Andy" Anderson (below). (Both, OCA.)

AERIAL VIEW OF KNOTT'S BERRY PLACE, 1947. An early 1947 aerial view shows visitors enjoying a typical day at Knott's Berry Place, with many visible buildings and attractions, including the Logging Wheels, the Ghost Town Grill, the Sheriff's Office, Goldie's Place, the Gold Trails Hotel, the Pitchur Gallery, the Blacksmith Shop, Betsy the Old Borax Engine, the Wells Fargo Express Office, the Bottle House, and the path to the Little Chapel by the Lake. Farther past Ghost Town (upper left), the construction of new buildings is underway.

Four

KNOTT'S BERRY FARM AND GHOST TOWN

THE KNOTT FAMILY, 1947. In mid-1947, Knott's Berry Place was renamed Knott's Berry Farm and Ghost Town, and business could not have been better for the Knott family—from left to right, Virginia, Cordelia, Walter, Russell, Marion, and Toni—as Ghost Town continued to thrive with even more entertaining buildings, attractions, and street performers.

Main Street, 1947. Ghost Town Main Street on any given day was packed with visitors, tourists, and families checking out the sights and attractions, and taking photographs to show their friends when they got home.

SLUMBERING INDIANS AND ADOBE RUINS, 1947. The Slumbering Indians (one leaning against the wall, the other sitting down) were two statues that were made by Knott's Berry Farm's resident sculptor, Claude Bell, in 1947 and placed at Adobe Corner, where they stood for many years next to the Adobe Ruins (below).

SAN FRANCISCO ARCHES, 1947. The San Francisco Arches were built in 1947 from adobe bricks and led to La Palma Avenue. In the 1970s, the arches became an old structure on the winding path where the Stagecoach Ride passed by. (OCA.)

JERSEY LILLY SALOON, 1947. The Jersey Lilly Saloon (Judge Roy Bean's) was built in 1947. Inside, visitors could order boysenberry punch and root beer. The saloon was a replica of the original, which was built in Texas in 1898 and named after actress Lillie Langtree. When Judge Roy Bean set up his saloon 200 miles away from the nearest town, he hung out a shingle, "Justice of the Peace," making it easier for rangers to bring culprits to him so he could dish out his own brand of Texas justice. (OCA.)

GOLD MINE, 1947. The Ghost Town Gold Mine was built in 1947 and was located to the left of the main entrance. Visitors could walk through the gold mine tunnel, and as they went farther down, streaks of glittering gold could be seen. (OCA.)

PAN FOR GOLD, 1947. Next to the Gold Mine, visitors enjoyed the popular Pan for Gold attraction, where they would line up next to an authentic sluice box and an experienced old-timer would demonstrate the proper way to pan for gold before letting them try it for themselves. When they spotted gold on the pan, it was placed in a souvenir bottle for a small fee. (OCA.)

HANDSOME BRADY AND WHISKEY BILL, 1947. Handsome Brady and Whiskey Bill were made by Claude Bell in 1947. These two concrete characters sat on the porch of the Gold Trails Hotel and through the years became two of the most photographed characters in the world. Bell was responsible for sculpting most of the life-size statues that were displayed all over Ghost Town.

GHOST TOWN FIRE STATION AND HANGMAN'S TREE, 1948. Using adobe bricks, the Ghost Town Fire Station was built in 1948 in front of the Gold Trails Hotel and housed the steam pumper, an old-time fire truck that had been fighting fires in New England since the 1880s. To the left of the station stood Hangman's Tree, with the remains of an old noose dangling from it.

CHIEF RED FEATHER, 1948. Chief Red Feather (Jim Urban Brady) worked as a boxer, marshal, rodeo rider, and actor before joining Knott's Ghost Town in 1948, becoming the most popular street performer in its history. He posed for pictures on Main Street and in front of the Bottle House for 35 years, and he sang, danced, and played the tom-tom in full regalia. (OCA.)

AUNT NELLIE, 1948. Aunt Nellie McKinney, from Missouri and already in her late 70s, came to Knott's Ghost Town in 1949, playing her dulcimer (a hammer-struck, trapezoidal musical instrument) on the porch of the Old Log Cabin and did so well into her 80s. The cabin was originally moved to Ghost Town from the Ozarks. The furnishings inside were typical of the way people lived in the West.

JO-AN BURDICK, 1948. Jo Burdick, from Anaheim, California, joined Knott's Berry Farm in 1948 as a junior hostess at the Chicken Dinner Restaurant, along with her sister, Wanda, who was already a waitress there. A year later, she moved over to the Steak House. In 1950, she auditioned and got the job as a can-can dancer at the Calico Saloon, where, at six-feet tall, she became one of the more popular dancers.

BUTTERFIELD STAGE LINE, 1949. The Butterfield Stage Line was started in 1949 by the white-bearded Bill Higdon (above) with just two horses and a covered wagon. Through the years, the stage line grew to have its own depot, four stagecoaches, and a covered wagon. By the mid-1950s, there were 30 fine horses, and as many as 70,000 passengers a month rode the line in the summertime. A fun part of the ride was when robbers would hold up the stagecoach and shoot off their pistols. (Both, OCA.)

COVERED WAGON CAMP, 1949. The Covered Wagon Camp, designed by Paul von Klieben, was built in 1949 just past the entrance to Ghost Town. It seated about 800 people and was encircled by 18 covered wagons to depict how the wagon trains circled their camp for protection from Native Americans. Each evening, a campfire was built in the center, and there was some kind of entertainment, be it Western music, singing cowboys, or square dancing.

BUD BOYDSTON, 1940s. Bud Boydston (on middle horse) joined Knott's Ghost Town in the late 1940s, and his main job was running the Covered Wagon Camp. Originally from Colorado, he was known as "the Wagon Master." He sang and played guitar, performing songs such as "Home on the Range" and "Let Me Call You Sweetheart." He hosted the musical acts that played at the Wagon Camp and was the square dance caller. (OCA.)

HARVEY WALKER, 1949. Harvey Walker joined Knott's Ghost Town in 1949 at the age of 15. Originally from Oklahoma, he worked in many capacities over the years, including train robber, undertaker, general store clerk, and popcorn wagon operator. He was also known for his incredible banjo playing. He later joined the Wagonmasters, who performed at the Covered Wagon Camp for many years.

DEE WOOLEM, 1949. Dee Woolem (in front) was a musician from Texas who first came to Knott's Ghost Town in 1949. In 1951, he started working as a train robber, later becoming one of the world's top fast-draw champions. He then went on to play bass for the Wagonmasters. (OCA.)

ROY BRYANT, 1940s. Roy Bryant was a farmer from Iowa who raised corn, cattle, and chickens before joining Knott's Ghost Town in the late 1940s as a miner conducting tours. He also lent atmosphere working as an old prospector, walking with his burro around Main Street, the Gold Mine, and the Prospector's Arastra. He would stop and have his picture taken with children, who always wanted to pet one of his burros.

MARK SMITH HORSE SHOW, 1950. The Mark Smith Horse Show opened in January 1950 in an enclosed arena on the outskirts of Calico Square (where the Calico Mine Ride was later built in 1960). Smith was a famous horse trainer with his own stables in Burbank, California, who was also known for his time with the Kellog's Horse Show. The arena seated 3,000 spectators and featured daring races and amazing horse tricks. It closed in 1955, as interest in the show dwindled. (OCA.)

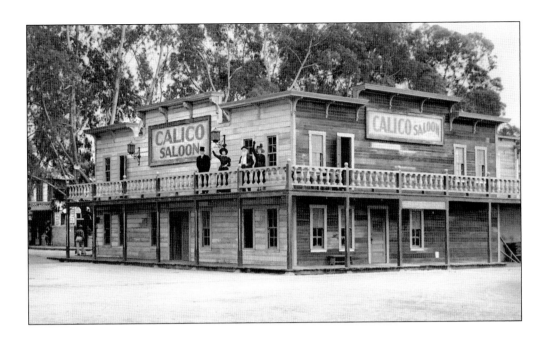

CALICO SALOON, 1951. The Calico Saloon (originally the Ghost Town Bar) was built in 1951 in Calico Square, incorporating many popular elements of old saloons throughout the West and serving sarsaparilla and boysenberry punch. It got its name because the saloon was lined with calico rather than wallpaper. Shows were presented daily, including Old West musicals, comedic entertainment, and a can-can show. The saloon also featured a massive painting behind the bar entitled *Saturday Night in Old Calico* by Paul von Klieben.

LES JONES, 1951. "Professor" Les Jones joined Knott's Ghost Town in 1949 and became the Calico Saloon's first piano player in 1951, accompanying the singers and can-can dancers during their popular shows. Originally from Graham, Texas, he first took up the accordion and then the piano, on which he was quite the showman. He also played the accordion alongside Bud Boydston in the Covered Wagon Camp. Jones's other roles included bartender at the Silver Dollar Bar and sheriff of Ghost Town.

MARILYN SCHULER AND CECELIA PETERSON, 1952. Marilyn Schuler (left) joined Knott's Ghost Town in 1951 as a can-can dancer at the Calico Saloon. Prior to that, she was a dance instructor. Cecelia Peterson (right) joined in 1952 as a singer and waitress at the Calico Saloon. With her big eyes and thick lipstick, she was a favorite among male patrons, especially servicemen on leave. Like most of the singers and dancers at the saloon, they both served boysenberry punch. Schuler and Peterson were photographed by visitors up and down Main Street throughout the 1950s and early 1960s. They were later immortalized by Claude Bell when their likenesses were built in a permanent monument in Calico Square.

ANITA DOVIE, 1950s. Anita Dovie, billed as "the Gold Rush Thrush," joined Knott's Ghost Town in the mid-1950s. Born in Anaheim, California, she trained as a classical singer and became one of the most well-known singers at the Calico Saloon. Her trademark routine included singing Gay Nineties songs, such as "Bird in a Gilded Cage" and "Oh You Beautiful Doll," all while holding a big fan. She later sang in the Church of Reflections until 1970.

PAUL SHEAK AND MADEMOISELLE MICHELE, 1950s. Paul Sheak (left) joined Knott's Ghost Town in the early 1950s. Originally from Germany, he had a background as a traveling showman and muscleman. In fact, besides working as a bartender at the Calico Saloon, he was known to rip a thick phone directory in half. He also had the unique talent of playing the musical saw. Michele Slaboda (right) was a can-can dancer and a protege of Jo Burdick.

BERT HANSEN, 1950s. "Banjo" Bert Hansen was an old showman who worked at Knott's Ghost Town throughout the 1950s and early 1960s, mostly from his Medicine Wagon (as Dr. Mal De Mer) selling his elixirs, but he would also walk around Ghost Town playing his banjo. His wife, Adele, worked in the Little Chapel by the Lake, the School House, and the General Store. (OCA.)

WALTER KNOTT RESTORES CALICO, 1951. In 1951, Walter Knott, because of his interest in American pioneer history, purchased Calico Ghost Town, an abandoned 70-acre silver mining town in San Bernardino County east of Barstow, and began rebuilding and restoring the town. In 1966, he deeded Calico to the County of San Bernardino as a recreational center and park. (OCA.)

MRS. MURPHY'S BOARDING HOUSE, 1951. Mrs. Murphy's Boarding House was moved to Knott's Ghost Town in 1951. It was originally the first post office in Downey, one of the oldest towns in Southern California. The animated figures inside the boardinghouse, built by the engineering department, depicted an old Thanksgiving family reunion. (Below, OCA.)

HARRY'S GUNSHOP, 1951. Harry's Gunshop opened in 1951 near the Post Office and was operated by Harry Durant and his wife, Dorotha. Along with a display of guns and rifles, handmade bows and arrows hung from the walls, and in the back of the shop was an archery range.

INDIAN VILLAGE, 1951. Indian Village was established on the island in Knott's Lake in 1951 after the trees had grown. It was started and operated by Frank Day and his wife, Ethel, and could be reached by bridge from the mainland. In the village, the Indian Store (Trading Post) carried an array of native merchandise and many valuable articles used in Native American ceremonials. (OCA.)

GHOST TOWN AND CALICO RAILWAY, 1951. The Ghost Town and Calico Railway was built in 1951. It was America's last operating narrow-gauge railroad from the 1880s, known as the Denver and Rio Grande, which was first built in 1871. When the Rio Grande Southern Railroad was placed on sale, Walter Knott purchased it and moved it in its entirety to Knott's Ghost Town. The rolling stock consisted of two locomotives, No. 40, "Gold Nugget" (above), and No. 41, "Red Cliff" (below), as well as two parlor cars, three coach cars, the president's car, and a caboose, which was used as a hangout by train robbers.

GOLDEN SPIKE CEREMONY, 1952. To celebrate the Ghost Town and Calico Railroad opening, Walter Knott hosted a golden spike ceremony in Calico Square to christen the railway on January 12, 1952, much to the delight of the huge crowd of onlookers. Speakers included Col. Ted Davis and actor Sterling Hayden, who drove in the spike. (OCA.)

ORIGINAL BERRY SHACK, 1952. The Original Berry Shack that Walter Knott sold his berries out of opened as an attraction in 1952, and boysenberry punch, coffee, and ice cream were still sold there. In front of the shack was a mounted plaque dedicated to the Knott family for all their years of hard work and perseverance. (OCA.)

GHOST TOWN SCHOOL, 1952. The Ghost Town School (the School House) was moved to Knott's Ghost Town on School House Road in 1952. It was originally built in 1876 in Beloit, Kansas, by a group of Iowa farmers who settled there in 1875. Walter Knott purchased it at auction, dismantled it, and had it trucked out to Ghost Town, where it was reconstructed, even replacing the original wooden nameplate above the door. Nina Duden was the first schoolteacher.

GRIST MILL, 1953. The gristmill from Yuba City, California, was built in 1953. Huge stones ground grain inside, and visitors could buy fresh-ground flour. Ray Gilkerson was the miller who ground the grains into meals and flours. Every morning, Walter Knott would go down to the mill, pick up some fresh grains, and bring them home, where his wife, Cordelia, would cook him oatmeal.

BOOT HILL CEMETERY, 1953. Boot Hill Cemetery was built in 1953 between the Grist Mill and the railroad tracks. Every mining town had to have a Boot Hill, and Ghost Town was no exception. Some of the old tombstones were authentic, while others were not, but every one of the epitaphs was from a real tombstone somewhere. (OCA.)

CHIEF OSAPANA, 1953. Chief Osapana (James "Ridge" Whiteman) joined Knott's Ghost Town in 1953, working as a carpenter and helping to build what would later be the Haunted Shack. Originally from New Mexico, he was half Powhatan and half Cherokee Indian. He worked at the farm for 20 years, first in the Indian Village taking pictures with visitors then later in the Calico Saloon, the Silver Dollar Bar, the Jersey Lilly Saloon, and the General Store.

CHIEF BLUE EAGLE, 1950s. Chief Blue Eagle joined Knott's Ghost Town in the early 1950s. Although he did not talk much, his job was to attract visitors to Indian Village and to shop inside the Trading Post. He also participated in the Medicine Show with Bert Hansen and Marilyn Schuler. (OCA.)

DREGER CLOCK, 1954. The Dreger Clock was installed in the Rose Garden at Knott's Berry Farm in 1954. This unusual piece was built by Long Beach watchmaker Andrew Dreger Sr., who started working on it in 1928 and spent five years completing it. It was an electrical piece, and many of the parts were hand tooled. It recorded the time, the day, the month, and the year. On one side, it had a series of little clocks set in a circle that give the time of day in 13 countries throughout the world. (OCA.)

MARILYN AND CECELIA, "THE CALICO BELLES," 1954. Marilyn and Cecelia, "the Calico Belles," were made by sculptor Claude Bell (above, kneeling) in 1954. These two concrete figures were placed on a platform in Calico Square and painted while they sat on their bench. The ladies were modeled after Marilyn Schuler and Cecelia Peterson, two popular performers in the Calico Saloon, and visitors flocked to sit with their concrete look-alikes and have their picture taken.

NIGHT WATCH STATUES, 1954. The Night Watch statues, consisting of a Native American warrior, his squaw, and their child, were made in 1954 and placed on the hills behind Boot Hill Cemetery, overlooking the stream and railroad trestle. They were sculpted by Ross Yost and were modeled after the famous *Night Watch* painting by Charles Nahl that hung in the Music Hall. (OCA.)

INDIAN ON THE HILL, 1954. The Indian on the Hill statue, which sent out smoke signals every night, was made in 1954 and placed on another hill on top of Boot Hill Cemetery. It was designed by the late Paul von Klieben and sculpted by Ross Yost.

OLD MINER PANNING FOR GOLD, 1954. The Old Miner Panning for Gold statue was made in 1954 and placed in the creek just below Boot Hill Cemetery. It was sculpted by Ross Yost.

MINER'S BANK, 1954. The Miner's Bank was built in 1954. The building was a replica and typical of many an early-day bank. The bank was located downstairs, while the E Clampus Vitus Lodge Hall (a typical ruin found in many ghost towns that sprang up during the Gold Rush) was located upstairs. Since the bank was not a real commercial bank, it was used by Edward Fish, a collector and dealer in old money, stamps, and gold. (OCA.)

HAUNTED SHACK, 1954. The Haunted Shack opened in June 1954, after Walter Knott purchased the shack from its original location in Esmeralda County, Nevada. Daily tours revealed the gravity-defying mysteries as told by Slanty Sam in "The Legend of the Haunted Shack." The wisecracking guide would walk visitors through a mysterious shack where water ran uphill, chairs balanced precariously on walls, and brooms stood on end. The shack was operated by Lester Wilson, who also designed its attractions.

BURRO RIDES, 1954. The Burro Rides (with 22 burros) opened in June 1954. Children loved to ride the small sturdy animals that were used as pack animals by miners in the Gold Rush days. The rides were owned and operated by Kenneth and Eva Johnson.

BIRD CAGE THEATRE, 1954. The Bird Cage Theatre opened in Knott's Ghost Town in 1954 as the home of the country's only daily acting melodrama troupe. Located next to the School House, the theater was a replica of the Bird Cage Theatre in Tombstone, Arizona. The owners of the theater were George Stuart and Woodie Wilson. Mae Mennes was the organ player and also played the calliope just outside the theater. (OCA.)

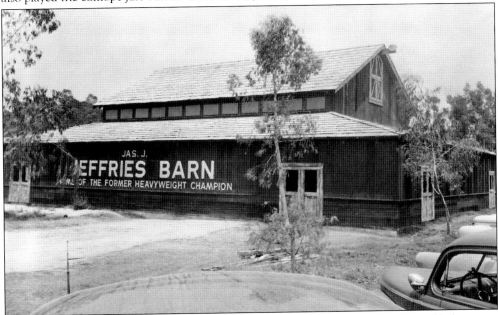

JIM JEFFRIES BARN, 1954. Jim Jeffries Barn was originally a dairy barn where world-champion boxer Jim Jeffries grew up and was later turned into a training camp for young boxers in Burbank, California. The barn was moved to the Knott's Berry Farm on Jeffries Street in November 1954 after the corner it stood on for many years was bought out. (OCA.)

SHIRLEY AND THE BEEMAN BROTHERS, 1939, AND THE WAGONMASTERS, 1955. The first music at Knott's Berry Farm was provided by Shirley and the Beeman Brothers (above) as early as 1939. In 1955, the Wagonmasters, founded by Dick Goodman, became the Covered Wagon Camp's main musical group, performing their western music there until 1968. The Wagonmasters had many members come and go throughout the years, but their 1960 lineup was quite memorable. Below, from left to right, are Eldon Eklund, Dave Bourne, Rachel Beeman, Vern Jackson, Billy Beeman, and Don Richardson. By the summer of 1968, the Wagonmasters had performed over 9,000 shows and put out half a dozen albums.

AERIAL VIEW OF KNOTT'S GHOST TOWN, 1954. A 1954 aerial view shows Knott's Ghost Town with many visible attractions and buildings, including the Horse Show Arena, the Ghost Town and Calico Railway, the Haunted Shack, the Calico Saloon, Boot Hill Cemetery, the Old Windmill, the Grist Mill, the Miner's Bank, and School House Road. (OCA.)

OLD MACDONALD'S FARM AND SEAL POOL, 1955. Old MacDonald's Farm opened in January 1955 just north of Indian Village, where ordinary farm animals did tricks, chickens rang the bell before going to lunch, rabbits rode cable cars, and goats butted Old MacDonald. The farm was owned and operated by Fulton Shaw. The Seal Pool, operated by C. W. Yeager, was located right next to the farm, and visitors could feed the seals with food purchased at the Seal Food Stand. (OCA.)

DENTZEL CAROUSEL, 1955. The Dentzel Carousel was the world's oldest working merry-go-round, built in 1896 in Pennsylvania by Tom Dentzel, who first introduced the merry-go-round to the United States. It was brought to Knott's Berry Farm in 1955 and placed just beyond Old MacDonald's Farm, where it was supervised by Bud Hurlbut, who would go on to become Knott's main ride designer. The carousel revolved to the strains of its antique band organ, with two chariot rides and 52 hand-carved animals. (OCA.)

CABLE CARS, 1955. The cable cars were put in operation on Easter Sunday, 1955. Walter Knott secured the four cars from San Francisco and brought them down to Knott's Berry Farm, where they were repainted. The cars were operated by means of large electric batteries, and they made daily trips on the mile track.

CHURCH OF REFLECTIONS, 1955. The Church of Reflections (originally built in Downey in 1876) was rebuilt at Knott's Berry Farm in 1955 and was moved across Beach Boulevard next to Reflection Lake. Walter Knott named it "Church of Reflections" because it gave all its visitors a serene, quiet place in which they might wish to meditate. It was the only known active church within an operating theme park.

MIDDLETON'S TRAIN SUPPLY HOUSE, 1955. Middleton's Train Supply House and Toy Museum opened in 1955 and was located across the street from Jim Jeffries Barn. This building housed a collection of over 4,000 items consisting of all types of iron toys, including model trains and trolleys dating back to 1860. The shop was owned by Evan Middleton, who with his wife, Frances, operated the model train sales and repair shop.

EL CAMINO REAL AND THE CALIFORNIA MISSIONS, 1950s. The San Diego Arches were built in the mid-1950s adjacent to Calico Square, near the Jersey Lilly Saloon. Soon afterwards, the arches were called "El Camino Real" and housed 21 miniature models representing the many California missions of the late 1700s. The models were created by renowned Italian artist Leon DeVolos and displayed inside an adobe wall behind glass. (Both, OCA.)

CHIEF WHITE EAGLE, 1956. Chief White Eagle was another popular street performer who worked at Knott's Ghost Town for 24 years, mostly up and down Main Street.

CANDY KITCHEN, 1956. At the Candy Kitchen, which opened in 1956, visitors were able to watch highly skilled candy makers craft a variety of candies and chocolates from scratch, such as suckers, candy canes, licorice sticks, and chocolate Easter bunnies. (OCA.)

PIONEERING PROSPECTOR AND BURRO, 1956. In 1956, the Pioneering Prospector and Burro monument, made from steel and concrete by Claude Bell (above) and Ross Yost, was placed atop a tall slab of rock at the main entrance at La Palma Avenue and the corner of Highway 39 (Beach Boulevard). Two other versions of the monument were also made. One was placed atop a slab of rock at the Western Avenue and La Palma Avenue entrance, and the other one could be found at the entrance to Ghost Town, near the Covered Wagon Camp. (Above, OCA.)

HENRY'S AUTO LIVERY, 1957.
Henry's Auto Livery opened in
July 1957 and was located out of
the main park near the corner of
Beach Boulevard and Crescent
Avenue. It had no tracks, just
bumpers to keep riders on the
road. The autos were designed
by Walter Beckman. (OCA.)

**MODEL T RIDES,
1957.** The Model
T Rides, for very
small children,
were added to the
farm in 1957 and
were located just
west of the Dentzel
Carousel. The five
authentic 1910
Ford Model Ts
were coin-operated
and did not go
anywhere, but
they shook, giving
youngsters the
sensation of driving,
with all the bumps
of an old-time
automobile. The
cars were made and
operated by Emory
Hoagland. (OCA.)

BILL HAZEL, 1957. Bill Hazel, from Mobile, Alabama, joined Knott's Ghost Town in 1957, first working as a prospector who led a set of burros through Ghost Town. He later worked in the Print Shop making "Wanted" posters and then down by the Goldmine, showing kids how to pan for gold. Hazel also practiced various gun-slinging tricks, like tossing his single-action Colt pistol in the air and catching it, ready for the draw.

WESTERN TRAILS MUSEUM, 1957. The Western Trails Museum, featuring the collection of lifelong Old West collector Marion Speers, moved from Liberty Park near Huntington Beach to Knott's Ghost Town in August 1957. Some of the more interesting artifacts displayed in glass cases were turn-of-the-20th-century rifles, guns, swords, spurs, soldier uniforms, branding irons, and a gold nugget exhibit. (OCA.)

RAINBOW TROUT FISHING AND HATCHERY, 1958. The Rainbow Trout Fishing and Hatchery, located at the Old Mill Stream, opened in March 1958 and was located on the southeast corner of Knott's Berry Farm. The lake was stocked with 18,000 rainbow trout, and catches were assessed at $1.50 per pound. Poles, bait, and buckets were free of charge. The concession was run by Ward McKalson and Cole Weston. (OCA.)

MOTT'S MINIATURES, 1958. Mott's Miniatures shop opened in Jim Jeffries Barn in 1958. The collection of over 150 miniature scenes, houses, and other Lilliputian displays was begun in 1911 by Allegra Mott (on right), who started collecting Cracker Jack prizes. Among other things, it showcased the development of the American home and the history of American merchandising. (OCA.)

MERRY-GO-ROUND AUTO RIDE, 1958. The Merry-Go-Round Auto Ride opened in June 1958. The cars followed an electrically activated track around curves, over bridges, and through tunnels while their drivers steered madly in a simulated attempt to keep the cars from running off the road. It was designed and built by Bud Hurlbut. (OCA.)

SHOOTIN' GALLERY, 1960. The Shootin' Gallery opened in July 1960 and was the first electronic shooting gallery in the country. It was developed by Italian immigrant Carlo Giannetti and his assistant, Martin Pincus, an electronics genius from Los Angeles. It took them two years to perfect the custom-made electronic guns, targets, and scenery. (OCA.)

CALICO MINE RIDE, 1960. The Calico Mine Ride opened to great fanfare in 1960. Designed and built by Bud Hurlbut (above), the ride was an ingenious trip into the depths of an Old West mine, climaxing with a loud, thunderous explosion. Its creative use of themed and special effects set a new standard for future Knott's attractions. Hurlbut also designed the miniature railroad engines in his own shop and arranged all the miners using a variety of mannequins. As visitors leave the train and travel down the walkway to the exit, they always stop for an instant and look back up at the mountain, as its solid rock face and roaring waterfalls tell little of the eight-minute adventure they just experienced. (Both, OCA.)

TONY KEMENY, 1960. Tony Kemeny, a Hungarian refugee and orphan who developed polio at an early age and survived the Dachau concentration camp, joined Knott's Berry Farm as a puppeteer in 1960, performing his puppet show at Fandango Hall and the Calico Saloon.

FIDDLIN' CHARLIE WAER, 1960s. Fiddlin' Charlie Waer played his fiddle all over Ghost Town from the early 1960s until the late 1970s. Originally from Kansas, he fiddled in front of the Gold Mine as well as on the porch of the Gold Trails Hotel, performing such standards as "My Darling Clementine." Kids would come up to him all the time, and he would help them hold the bow, guiding them through a song.

PROSPECTOR'S DAY, 1963. Prospector's Day was celebrated at Knott's Berry Farm once a year from 1959 to 1973 to commemorate the discovery of gold in California. The ceremonies included a parade through the streets of Ghost Town, and Walter and Cordelia Knott (couple on left) presided over the festivities and greeted visitors. (OCA.)

STEVE KNOTT, 1963. In 1963, Steven Knott (Russell's son) returned to Knott's Berry Farm from a stint in the U.S. Army and was assigned to the security department, which he eventually ran. As a young teenager, "Little Stevie" worked in many capacities, including street sweeper, opening and closing the chapel doors, general store clerk, Berry Market clerk, chicken truck helper, grounds crew, Steak House crew, and Preserving Kitchen helper. (OCA.)

CORDELIA K. STEAMBOAT, 1963. The *Cordelia K.* steamboat was built by Bud Hurlbut in 1963 and was added to Knott's Lake in August. John Holland of the stage lines helped in its design. (OCA.)

JUNGLE ISLAND, 1964. Jungle Island was created in the Lagoon area on the east side of Highway 39 in 1964, and the entrance to the island was gained through a bridge where the pathways were filled with carved wooden figures called "Wood-imals." The figures, created by Forrest Morrow using branches and trunks of trees, were brought to Knott's Berry Farm from Morrow's home in Elgin, Illinois.

OVERLAND TRAIL RIDE, 1964. The Overland Trail Ride opened in May 1964 and took passengers out on a carriage ride led by a pair of sturdy draft horses, winding through the back ways and canyons where visitors could catch a glimpse of Mother Nature's wild animals, including a coyote watching over her cub and a big black bear named Bruin. The ride, which lasted seven minutes, was developed by John Holland. (OCA.)

ROY ROGERS AND DALE EVANS SHOW, 1964. *The Roy Rogers and Dale Evans Show*, which aired on KABC Channel 7, filmed the popular one-hour network show at Knott's Ghost Town in 1964. Featured on the show were the Sons of the Pioneers, Cliff Arquette, the Smothers Brothers, and of course, Roy's horse, Trigger. Scenes included stops at the School House, the Gun Shop, the Train Depot, and the Livery Stable.

INDEPENDENCE HALL, 1966. In 1966, Walter Knott completed construction on a brick-by-brick replica of Independence Hall, complete with a cracked 2,075-pound Liberty Bell built by Bud Hurlbut. An audio presentation, with speakers located at appropriate tables, recalled the debate that led to the Declaration of Independence. (OCA.)

DEAN DAVISSON, 1966. Dean Davisson became the spokesperson for Independence Hall in 1966. He was hired by Russell Knott back in 1948 as Knott's Berry Farm's director of public relations and held that position until 1976, when he retired. For 28 years, Davisson handled all press requests for television, commercials, and motion pictures. (OCA.)

WALTER KNOTT IN HIS OFFICE, 1960s. Walter Knott would spend countless hours in his office with his wife, Cordelia, by his side, coming up with new ideas on how to improve Knott's Berry Farm and make it more enjoyable and entertaining. (OCA.)

THE KNOTT FAMILY, 1960s. By the late 1960s, Walter Knott's family had become more involved in the daily operations of Knott's Berry Farm, with each member handling a specific department and being fully entrusted to run it to the best of their capabilities. From left to right are Russell and Mildred Knott; Virginia Knott Reafsnyder; Darrel Anderson with his parents, Dwight and Marion Knott Anderson; Steve and Ken Knott, Russell's sons; Ken and Toni Knott Oliphant; and (in front) Walter and Cordelia Knott.

BIG CROWDS AT KNOTT'S BERRY FARM, 1968. A significant change for Knott's Berry Farm occurred on June 5, 1968, when repeated vandalism forced the Knotts to erect a fence around their 200-acre amusement park, and for the first time, they began charging admission. Once visitors had to pay an admission fee, they expected to be entertained the way they were at Disneyland, and indeed they were, as the crowds became bigger and bigger. (OCA.)

MARION KNOTT ANDERSON. Between 1968 and 1975, under the guidance of Marion Knott Anderson (Walter Knott's daughter), who had assumed creative control of the family business in 1968, Knott's Berry Farm launched a $17-million expansion that saw the remodeling and addition of many new themed areas. (OCA.)

FIESTA VILLAGE, 1969. Fiesta Village was added to Knott's Berry Farm in 1969. It was the first new themed area conceived by Marion Knott Anderson. The village was a tribute to early Spanish architecture, with adobe buildings, tile roofs, and colorful hand-decorated title walls, which reflected a culture dating back to the 16th century. The Mexican-themed area also featured a number of carnival-style rides including the Tijuana Taxi, the Mexican Whip, and the Fiesta Wheel.

CALICO LOG RIDE, 1969. The Calico Logging Company opened in 1969. This exciting new log ride took visitors around twisting turns, showing turn-of-the-20th-century lumberjacks (mannequins) working on a lumber mill and presenting a first-hand view of each phase of a logging operation, highlighted by a 75-foot drop at its conclusion. The ingenious ride was designed and built by Bud Hurlbut, and was one of the first log flume rides in the United States. The opening ceremonies were attended by John Wayne and his son Ethan, who were the first to ride it. (Both, OCA.)

GYPSY CAMP, 1971. Gypsy Camp opened in June 1971 and was the second themed area conceived by Marion Knott Anderson. Its 3-acre encampment was situated among man-made mountains, flaming torches, and Gypsy caravans. The main attraction in Gypsy Camp was the John Wayne Theatre, named after the famous actor and longtime family friend. Unfortunately, the camp never caught on with visitors and was hastily closed in 1974. (OCA.)

KNOTT'S SCARY FARM, 1973. The first Knott's Scary Farm Halloween celebration took place in 1973 and has been drawing big crowds ever since. The event was created by Bill Hollingshead and Gary Salisbury. "Sinister Seymour" (Larry Vincent), a local television horror-show personality, served as the first celebrity host of the event in 1973.

WILD WEST STUNT SHOW, 1974. The Wild West Stunt Show, which opened in the Covered Wagon Camp in 1974, originally began as "the Funfighters on the Streets of Ghost Town," created by Gary Salisbury in 1971. The stunt show's basic premise was that a member of the audience was chosen to come on stage, all the while trying to avoid being gunned down from a tall building by a mean stuntman as the show's host demonstrated various fighting techniques.

CORDELIA KNOTT PASSES AWAY, 1974. Cordelia Knott died on April 23, 1974, at the age of 84 and was buried in Loma Vista Cemetery in Fullerton, California. Afterwards Walter Knott turned his attention toward political causes, leaving day-to-day park operations to his children. (OCA.)

ROARING TWENTIES, 1975. The Roaring Twenties opened in 1975 and was the third themed area conceived by Marion Knott Anderson, featuring many new exciting rides, including the 360-degree roller coaster Corkscrew, the Wheeler Dealer Bumper Cars, and Knott's Bear-y Tales. In 1976, Knott's Airfield was added, which included the 20-story Parachute Sky Jump and Sky Cabin, the Motorcycle Chase, the Loop Trainer Flying Machine, the Propeller Spin, the Whirlpool, and the Whirlwind. (OCA.)

WALTER KNOTT DIES AT AGE 91, 1981. Walter Knott lived in a double-wide trailer inside the farm until his death on December 3, 1981, one week before his 92nd birthday. He was buried at Loma Vista Cemetery in Fullerton, California, next to his beloved wife.

Five

VINTAGE KNOTT'S MEMORABILIA

BOYSENBERRY PIE TIN, 1940S. A favorite pastime of many Americans is collecting old items and souvenirs from the many places they have visited throughout their life. Knott's Berry Farm and Ghost Town has no shortage of vintage items, collectibles, and memorabilia, going as far back as the early 1930s with the first Tea Room menu. A boysenberry pie tin from the 1940s is very significant in Knott's history, as they were specifically used to bake Cordelia Knott's pies and were sold at the Chicken Dinner Restaurant.

BOYSENBERRY PUNCH DRINKING CUP, 1950s. Boysenberry punch was sold at Knott's Berry Farm going as far back as the mid-1940s and was a favorite with all visitors. The punch was also available from the Original Berry Stand in the 1950s. The small drinking cups that were used to sell the punch were typically thrown away after being used. Some, however, have been saved in their original condition.

POPCORN BAG, 1950s. Popcorn was a favorite snack at Knott's Berry Farm in many different locations around Ghost Town during the 1940s, 1950s, and 1960s, as vendors sold it from a colorful popcorn wagon. The popcorn bags came in two sizes, small and large.

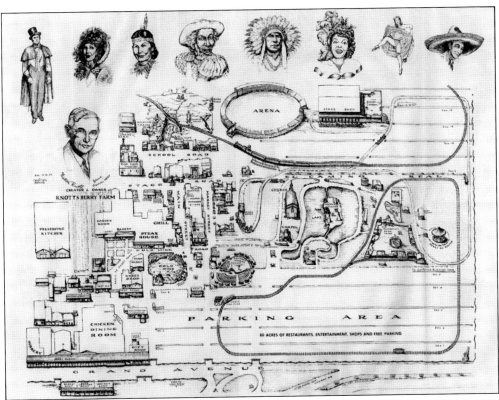

SOUVENIR MAP, 1950s. Souvenir brochures with detailed maps on the back have been given away at Knott's Berry Farm since the early 1950s. On one side would be a list of attractions and shops, while the other side contained a neatly sketched map of where visitors could walk, shop, and enjoy themselves. After more than 50 years, it is fun to see where many of the old attractions and shops used to be located.

BUTTERFIELD STAGE LINE TICKET, 1950s. During the 1950s and early 1960s, visitors to Knott's Berry Farm and Ghost Town needed to purchase separate tickets to go on a specific ride, with different prices for both adults and children. One such ticket was for the Butterfield Stagecoach Ride, which contained neat information about the ride with some make-believe details to give it authenticity.

125

COVERED WAGON SHOW 3-D CARD, 1940S. The Covered Wagon Show, which told the story of Walter Knott's grandparents and their journey west by wagon train, was a popular attraction in the Gold Trails Hotel for many years. In the mid-1940s, a three-dimensional souvenir card was handed out after the show that was a replica of the large cyclorama painting inside the hotel. It is one of the most interesting souvenirs ever sold at Knott's Ghost Town.

ASHTRAY, 1950S. During the 1940s, 1950s, and 1960s, the General Merchandise Store and other shops at Knott's Berry Farm always had a number of different ashtrays for sale. The ashtrays would usually have an old prospector, a stagecoach, or a boysenberry painted on them, along with the words "Knott's Berry Farm and Ghost Town."

BIBLIOGRAPHY

Bailey, Paul and Roger Holmes. *Fabulous Farmer: The Story of Walter Knott and His Berry Farm.* Los Angeles: Westernlore Publishers, 1956.

Bourne, Dave. "Knott's Berry Farm's Ghost Town." Agoura Hills, CA: SaloonPiano.com, 2006.

Brigandi, Phil. "Breaking New Ground: The Early Years of Knott's Berry Farm." *The Branding Iron* (Summer 2008).

Knott, Walter. *Calico Ghost Town.* Buena Park, CA: Knott's Berry Farm, 1959.

———. *Ghost Town and Calico Railway.* Buena Park, CA: Knott's Berry Place, 1953.

———. *Ghost Town History and Reference.* Buena Park, CA: Knott's Berry Farm, 1955.

———. *Ghost Town News, Souvenir Edition.* Buena Park, CA: Knott's Berry Farm, 1943.

———. *Knott's Berry Farm and Ghost Town.* Buena Park, CA: Knott's Berry Farm, 1949.

———. *Knott's Berry Farm and Ghost Town, Souvenir Edition.* Buena Park, CA: Knott's Berry Farm, 1976.

———. *The Knotty Post.* Buena Park, CA: Knott's Berry Farm, 1949–1975.

———. *The Story Of Knott's Berry Farm and Ghost Town.* Buena Park, CA: Knott's Berry Farm, 1954.

Kooiman, Helen. *Walter Knott: Keeper of the Flame.* Fullerton, CA: Plycon Press, 1973.

Norris, R. Frank. A Live Ghost Town: Story of the World Famous Knott's Berry Farm and Ghost Town. Buena Park, CA: Knott's Berry Farm, 1950.

Nygard, Norman. *Walter Knott: Twentieth Century Pioneer.* Grand Rapids, MI: Zondervan Publishing House, 1965.

DISCOVER THOUSANDS OF LOCAL HISTORY BOOKS FEATURING MILLIONS OF VINTAGE IMAGES

Arcadia Publishing, the leading local history publisher in the United States, is committed to making history accessible and meaningful through publishing books that celebrate and preserve the heritage of America's people and places.

Find more books like this at
www.arcadiapublishing.com

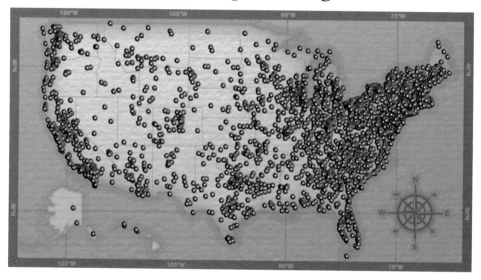

Search for your hometown history, your old stomping grounds, and even your favorite sports team.

Consistent with our mission to preserve history on a local level, this book was printed in South Carolina on American-made paper and manufactured entirely in the United States. Products carrying the accredited Forest Stewardship Council (FSC) label are printed on 100 percent FSC-certified paper.

MADE IN THE USA